The Condor of Chavín

A Journey in the Peruvian Andes

By Sam Woolsey

Take the road less traveled

ISBN 10: 1720701466
ISBN-13: 978-1720701460

ACKNOWLEDGEMENTS

Ann Marie Woolsey, Trish Neal, Gail Sheckley,
CeeCee Anderson, Kim McCullough,
and Josephine Dana

.

CONTENTS

Chapter 1:
Yungay, Ancash, Peru – Day 1

No story I could ever invent would be as gripping as this venture in 1979 into the Peruvian Andes.

Something held me fast as I sat in an old bus meandering its way through the green hills of the Cordillera Blanca Mountain range in northern Peru. I couldn't really put a finger on it, but the strength of it was enough to make me aware of fear and overwhelming solitude. I couldn't move and began to break out in a nervous sweat. I sat there trying to analyze where it was coming from and realized that it was coming from within me.

Anxiety; I was filled with it, and a knowledge that I would soon be once again placing myself into the jaws of fate and trekking out into the unknown in search of God knows what. Some people call it "experience" or "knowledge," others "adventure," but I term it insanity. I mean, what else could you call it? Especially since I had just left the most incredibly comfortable situation I had found in Peru, living in a luxurious hacienda compound for $2.50 a day and being treated like a fat cat by the young women who worked there. An easier situation I don't think could be found anywhere. I guess maybe the word "easier" is a clue to this mindless action on my part. Somewhere inside of me a feeling of action had to be satisfied. Luxuriating in the Garden of Eden had taken its toll and I yearned for something to challenge me physically and mentally. And "that something" would have to be intense enough to approximate the intensity of the Garden. Here's what I had written in my journal a few days earlier about this feeling of luxury which accurately describes part of what it was like.

Chancos Banos

There is something about sitting in a garden that tranquilizes the senses. The eyes have nothing to look upon but colors that blaze and tantalize, making it easy to drift along oblivious to outside realities. The nostrils fill with pungent odors that block out the offensive smells of the street. The ears can easily muffle city traffic, taking in and turning onto purer forms of natural harmonies that only airborne creatures can generate. Such it is that I'm sitting in one of those proverbial Gardens of Eden in this small community of Huaraz, high in the Cordillera Blanca of the Andes Mountains. Soft, even the rain is not offensive since it doesn't demand the subjection of the total environment to its bosom. Instead it allows the sun its due for the better part of the day and doesn't make itself known until the waning hours of the afternoon and on into the evening, leaving when the sun bursts upon the scene the following morning. This environment is not completely natural since it is cultivated and cared for by attentive gardeners who work daily all year round.

From columnar pillars at the entrance of the garden, a walkway composed of glass bottle bottoms stretches through the garden to a giant tree in a large marble planter at the end. Roses of different colors and sizes are planted here and there in the grass. The garden itself is about 50' X 100' in size, and it is only one of several that are in the expansive grounds of the Hostal Colomba, owned and operated by Señora Colomba, a gracious woman of obvious wealth who nonetheless is generous and quite gregarious. She is charging me 500 soles ($2.50) for a two-bed bungalow, one of at least 50 that are surrounded by a forest of landscaped pine trees. It is very easy to be relaxed here, and I am.

Pathway to Bungalows at Hostal Colomba

Mural at Hostal Colomba

And so, it was that I left these surroundings to blend the Ying with the Yang. I went from the luxury of comfort to the luxury of discomfort, from a soft bed to the hard ground. What a trade-off. My mind was furious, but my spirit soared as I anticipated a week-long trek into the highest mountains of Peru and some of the most beautiful country in the world. Trekking to heights of 18,000 feet and passing between 20,000 foot peaks, I knew that this would be one of those insane, irresponsible ventures that would leave luxurious memories indelibly etched in my mind.

It was still early morning, the sun just beginning to show its face over the eastern hills. The bus wound its way up through the Callejon de Huaylas Valley on this narrow blacktop road passing small hamlets where the inhabitants were busy working in the fields. I watched and wondered how it must be for these campesinos. Surrounded by incredibly high mountains and lush terrain, I was tempted to idealize their situation, but I knew that hardship was the reality of their existence. Especially here in the Callejon de Huaylas, situated under the watchful eye of Mt. Huascaron, where disaster was only an earthquake away.

It was here in 1970, in the early morning hours, that an earthquake destroyed a half dozen towns, killing 70,000 people, including most of the population of Yungay which had 20,000 sleeping people that morning. The side of the mountain split apart and within minutes traveled the few miles to Yungay, burying it under a mountain of dirt. There was nothing left, just dirt and rock.

Artistic Representation of the Andes

I realized this as we arrived just a few miles near the "new" town of Yungay. The bus slowed as we entered the city limits, and I knew immediately by the newness of everything, that something had happened here. The road went from narrow blacktop to a wide thoroughfare with concrete curbs and a divider in the middle. All the buildings were new white-washed adobe, international aid written all over them.

I got out of the bus and looked around, trying to gain a sense of direction. I saw a sign on a building pertaining to Mt. Huascaron National Park and headed for it. There was a man sitting at a new desk inside and I tapped on the sliding glass window to get his attention. He opened it smiling and asked what I needed. I inquired about the time that the bus left for the park and he said that it had already left. I swore to myself but wasn't to be put off and asked if there was any other way to get there. He looked out onto the street where a truckload of peasants sat in the back end of a dump truck and told me to catch a ride with them. I thanked him, grabbed my pack and sleeping bag that I had rented the day before for this venture and ran for the truck just as it was pulling away from the curb. The driver stopped, and with a little coaxing from my wallet I managed to secure a couple of feet in the back for my belongings and myself. We were at least twenty people back there, crammed together in intimate association. These guys were all workers on the road that was being built over the high pass between Huascaron and the other mountains in the National Park. The road would eventually tie the Callejon de Huaylas Valley with the Piscobamba Highway, some eighty or more kilometers to the east.

The truck headed back out of town in the direction I had just come from and then turned on a gravel road which led toward the mountains. As we climbed up this zig-zagging road toward the park, I looked back toward Yungay and saw the one memorial placed where the old town had been located. It was a white statue of the Madonna standing on top of the most prominent point in the area. There were no other signs of a town ever having been there. It was just dirt and big boulders, as if it had been the remnants of an ancient glacier that had receded back into the mountains. In fact, the road followed the path of the giant slide for the entire ten kilometers to the park itself. I sat in the back of the truck and felt a chill, and I thought of the fine line between living and dying. One of the girls working at the Hostal Colomba where I had been staying in Huaraz lost her whole family in Yungay. My heart went out to Violetta and the suffering that she has had to endure. It is always the ones left behind who must cope with the pain of loss.

Violetta in Hostal Colomba

After an hour or so of enduring a sore ass from bouncing all over the road, we finally came to the park entrance. The truck stopped and let me off and then continued on up the road to the job site at the top of the pass. I was met by a park ranger who took me into a small shack where I signed a form saying where I planned to go and how long I planned to stay. My plans were to spend a few days in the park, taking the Indian trail that went over an 18,000-foot pass, and then hiking out of the park towards the Rio Negra Valley and the town of Llumpa where a road passed through and bus service was available to take me out of the mountains. All in all, I planned to spend four or five days trekking out there, taking on whatever the fates had to throw at me.

I came out of the shack, grabbed my pack, bade adios to the park ranger, and then headed up the road toward Lake Llanganuco, described as a beautiful emerald lake fed by the glaciers from the high peaks that surround it. I was now hiking out of the lowlands and into the high-walled domain of Andean giants.

As I climbed higher along the road, I continued to move deeper into the yawning narrows of the high walls that closed in on me. They stretched up on both sides a thousand feet or more, with ribbons of water cascading down from their tops. The minerals in the water discolored the gray face of the basalt with yellows, greens and aquamarines. As I climbed higher, the canyon narrowed to where the base of the mountains on both sides was only a stone's throw away.

Upper Llanganuco Valley

I could see above that the road came to an apex, and I figured that the lake must be up there somewhere. And so, it was after another half hour I found myself at one end of a glacial valley surrounded by giant snow-capped peaks. There, directly in front of me, was an incredibly beautiful emerald lake set here over 14,000 feet above sea level. Except for a few groves of deciduous trees and green meadows surrounding the lake, it was a land of receding glaciers. My eyes followed these rivers of rock as they carved paths through the land making their way up to the mountains surrounding me, another 6,000 feet higher.

Lake Llanganuco

[From where I stood the snow line was still at least 3,000 to 4,000 feet farther up. I guess this is typical of the tropical Andes. Being so much closer to the equator than the high mountains of North America, they have a proportionately higher freezing level. The breathing wasn't too difficult yet, probably because I had been living at 11,000 feet for the last few weeks, but I still had an 18,000-foot pass to negotiate the next day.

I imagine that by my description of this place, it would seem that few men ever ventured here and those that did only by foot, well, "It ain't necessarily so." After all, I did climb a gravel road to get here, so sure enough I wasn't the only one up here. There was a parking lot close to where I was standing, and it held three or four cars. The people were all Peruvians and they weren't interested in much other than standing in front of the lake having their pictures taken with their cameras. These guys were more likely from Lima and staying in Huaraz for a few days. Because there wasn't any place to stay at the lake and since they didn't look like campers, I knew that serenity would soon be mine. Sure enough, after the women had posed numerous times beside the lake and then the car, and after they had drunk their Inca Colas, eaten their potato chips, and dangled their feet in the water, it was time for them to go. That was just fine with the men, since there weren't any cantinas up here where a guy could get a cold beer and maybe some fried chicken. So, they all got in their little VW's or Datsuns or whatevers and turned around, heading

Road from Lake Llanganuco

back for civilization and all of its accoutrements. Actually, this scene could be one found anywhere in the world. Tourists are tourists: city people that have a hard time functioning when they are more than five blocks from a 7-11 store. Or in this case, from a wood shacked *tienda*. Of course, in their minds I was probably an elitist in my thinking, since I would rather keep places like this for myself and people who thought like I did. I was fast finding myself relating more with the poor campesinos, who had to walk the distances between points, while the rich, white Peruvians drove through, but never seemed at ease with the wilds of their own country. I couldn't imagine anything more untouched or beautiful.

The air was crisp and moist, as clouds that weren't there a half hour before quickly moved down out of the mountains and threatened to engulf me. Maybe those tourists knew something I didn't. I quickly decided that I had better seek shelter and so grabbed my pack and walked around the parking lot toward a building to one side of it that looked abandoned. I thought I was in luck only to find a park ranger barring the door to this empty "chicken coup."

He asked me for my permit to stay there. I told him that I had already signed in at the park headquarters back down the road, but that didn't seem to make any impression upon him. He said that it was impossible to stay here without a permit, so I accepted my fate and handed

Road from Lake Llanganuco in the clouds.

him 1,000 soles or $5.00, which opened the door to this abandoned hovel immediately. I was just glad to have shelter from the potentially ominous weather that was quickly surrounding me. It wasn't long before it started to rain, and everything was socked in. So, I sat in my "suite," which consisted of a concrete floor with one broken-back chair for furniture and tried to wish away the hours that I had to spend until morning. Since it was only 7:00 p.m., the hours were going to be difficult to wish away very speedily. With one candle to light the ever-pervading darkness, I ate a few candy bars and watched the shadows dance along the four walls. Actually, I really didn't mind that much, since I could have been out in that rain instead, with only a sleeping bag for shelter. It was accurate to say that I really wasn't prepared for harsh or even mild weather conditions. The sleeping bag and pack I had were rented from an outfitter the day before were all he had left, so it's easy to imagine what kind of shape they were in. Oh, well, I was an optimist and figured I could survive on perseverance alone.

The candle flickered and burned, strangely lulling me into a sleep that actually lasted for an hour or two. The rest of the night was spent somewhere in a limbo between sleep and lucidity. I kept dreaming that I was lying on concrete of all things. After what seemed an eternity, a faint hint of light came through a window. Upon noticing this, I no longer attempted to carry on the myth of sleeping and got up. I looked through my bag for a candy bar that I had packed the day before, and instead placed my hands on something quite different. I really hadn't planned too well for this trip, figuring on staying in the local villages along the way, which would allow me to travel lightly. Consequently, I didn't have much packed. To my surprise, I found that some good fairy, namely Violeta, had packed my bag full of sandwiches, boiled eggs, dried meat, and a few other edibles. I think she liked me, and my good impressions of her were reinforced. So, I ate a full meal, washed up, and then loaded my pack, threw it over my shoulders and headed out into the dawn.

Sam Woolsey

CHAPTER 2:

YANAMA, ANCASH, PERU – DAY 2

It was still raining slightly, but not enough to dampen my enthusiasm for the hike to come. I got back on the gravel road and watched as the area began to open up in front of me. The lake moved past me on my right as I came to the top of a small hill. To my delight, I came upon another emerald lake which fed into Llanganuco.

Everywhere else it was rocks, boulders, and short grass for what must have been five or more miles. The road led to a wall at the far end of this glacial bowl where I knew I had to hike up and over a pass between the high peaks. The mountains poked up through the clouds on all sides. The largest, Huascaran, stood a head higher than the rest. What a beautiful sight. I could easily see why this was one of the most popular areas in the world for alpinists.

As I walked along the gravel road through this bowl of glaciated giants, a familiar sense of well-being rose within me that always seemed to accompany my excursions. Whether here in the mountains of Peru, the Himalayas of Nepal, or on Mt. Hood in Oregon, to be out in the wilderness of nature was to be a step closer to perfection. I felt the exhilaration of a man communing with that which makes his soul stir.

I had hiked for one or two hours and found myself closing in on the wall which stood as a barrier to further progress. I knew that somehow a trail meandered up from there to the 18,000-foot level and then over the pass. I wasn't prepared for the fact that the road continued up as well. I thought it would end at the bottom. But no, the road snaked its way up and up, 4,000 feet, to the top of the pass. It wasn't long after this revelation that a truck full of workers came along. They stopped and offered to take me to the top of the pass. My spirit refused to be compromised, but a beseeching cry from my feet for respite from the constant pounding against the gravel, overrode my purer thoughts, and we found ourselves (my feet and I) in the back end of this flat-bed truck with 20 other workers climbing to the top of the pass. I was glad the truck showed up, because it would have been a long climb, and I still had to hike for two or three hours once I was over the pass just to get to the first village. So, up and up we went. The clouds gathered in to greet us, carrying rain naturally, thankfully no snow, not even at the top of the pass. I could see that the snow line was still about a thousand feet above the pass.

At the top, the road ended. I got out and paid the driver 100 soles for the trip. I looked around for a trail, walking awkwardly through the road construction, trying not to make a fool of myself by falling in the muck or stumbling into something I shouldn't. Finally, a woman straw boss pointed me in the right direction, and I climbed up over an embankment and up the last 100 feet of the pass to find the trail at the top. It was raining hard now, and the Indios trail had a small gorge running down through the middle of it. I couldn't make out the countryside very well for all the clouds that surrounded me but figured I would eventually find my way.

I wasn't the only one up here either. I was constantly being passed by more agile *campesinos* loaded down with

Mt. Huascaran

fruit and vegetables from Yungay. Most of them didn't have much for shoes, but my new Vibram soled hiking boots didn't seem to make much difference. A lesser man would have found his ego bruised, but not me, no sir. I was too busy concentrating on the pain that was shooting from my oh-so-soft feet, to think about the irony of it all. I just kept my nose to the ground, winding on down the hill toward the first village. After a while my feet got a second wind, and I also found that I was getting below the clouds.

It was about this time that a lone *campesino,* leading a laden-down horse behind him, came up behind me. He slowed down, keeping pace with me. We soon found ourselves trying to communicate. He knew about as much

Mt. Huascaran in the clouds

Spanish as I did which made it easier to understand each other, since our vocabulary and tense use were about the same; simple. We started by exchanging names; his being Francisco and his horse; Walter.

Francisco became a hit with me immediately. Anybody who would name his horse "Walter" had to have a sense of humor. Another friendly trait of Francisco's was that he loved to laugh. Everything I had to say was a real joy to him. Even my name, Samuel, produced a guffaw or three. We passed the next three hours walking, laughing, and exchanging words in his native Quechua and my English.

At first, our focus was placed on plants and animals that we happened across. Soon, Francisco veered toward another subject so often discussed between two men; women. He was very eager to describe his wife as he sculpted a picture with his hands that covered her from head to toe. He impressed me as a man who was proud of his mate and easily swayed toward conversation about her. He also sculpted two smaller figures, his face beaming with the pride of a young father.

He then asked about my wife, of which I told him I had none. He looked surprised at this, especially since he had been married for four years. He was 19, while I was turning 30 that year. All I could say in reply to this was that I wasn't ready to settle down and hadn't met the right woman anyway but hoped someday to make a move in that direction. There were too many places to go and people to meet. My friend, who had never been to Lima, couldn't relate.

This conversation advanced us a couple of hours down the trail, and it seemed like we ought to be fast moving upon Francisco's village. He got on top of Walter, deciding to ride on ahead to his house where he insisted that I spend the night. How could I refuse, especially since I knew nowhere else to stay? So, he rode on and I kept walking, and walking, and walking, until I could barely move for the blisters and hot points on the bottom of my feet. Finally, I came around one last bend and saw the village of Yanama another 300 yards away. Those last 300 yards were probably the longest I had ever hiked.

As I entered Yanama, my arrival was announced by every dog in the vicinity. To be a gringo was to be a celebrity, even to these scrawny curs. All eyes settled on me as I moved into town. They weren't unfriendly stares, and smiles were easily found, especially from the small children. It wasn't long before Francisco found me and led me up a trail, above the center of town where he had a store and a house with a barnyard in between. The store consisted of a 4x6 foot room from which he sold salt. There was no table, and the only furniture consisted of some planks of wood laying on top of flat rocks that bordered the inside walls of the room. I soon found as I stood around that this was one of the local spots for the men to lounge in. They sat on the wood planks, lit cigarettes and talked about the happenings around town. I was one of those happenings, and Francisco had a great time as my benefactor, telling everyone all about me as if we were close friends. I loved it. The men listened to his every word as gospel, nodding and looking at me as one would when in the presence of a mysterious foreigner. I took it that not many gringos pass this way through the Andes.

Soon I decided to up the ante a bit and pulled out my 35mm Pentax to see what kind of a reaction I would get. There was great interest in the camera itself but not much for the idea of having their pictures taken. I turned to Francisco standing in the doorway that led to the barnyard. I asked if he would like to have a picture of his family. His ready smile answered the question, and soon we were all outside standing in a field.

His wife held their youngest, and an older son stood next to her with Francisco beside them. Then came a few more friends, and soon we had a real extended family

Francisco and family

portrait with grins abounding. After this, Francisco stood with "Walter" for a private portrait of the two amigos. Walter looked proud by Francisco's side.

That evening, Francisco brought some sheep hides into the store, laying them on the floor for me to sleep on that night. It wasn't the "Ritz," but it was shelter. Soon after, he came in with the first course of what was to be a three-course meal. It was a sort of soupy gruel made from potatoes. After a long day of hiking, I didn't think anything could have tasted better! About fifteen minutes later, he popped in the doorway with the second course, which turned out to be baked potatoes, salted of course. At this point I began to realize the extent of poverty that this man really knew. Something struck inside of me, and I asked Francisco if it would be alright if I could see his house. He said of course, and we went out through Walter's barnyard to the house a few meters away.

The two Amigos: Walter and Francisco

There was a faint light coming from an open doorway through which I lowered my head and entered. I found the entire family sitting in what was the only room of the house, on the only piece of furniture that I could see. It was a high, long bench that had sheep hides over it for a cushion. A small fire in the middle of the earthen floor was the only light and warmth they had. The walls were adobe clay with a few religious pictures adorning them. In one corner of the room a candle flickered, illuminating a small shrine of the Madonna with child.

A little embarrassed upon entering the sanctity of their home, I thanked them all for having put me up for the evening and wished to pay them something for their hospitality. To this I found the pride of poverty throwing up a wall in front of me which forbade any further talk of this kind. Of course, I wouldn't pay. I was their guest, and that's all there was to it.

So, the subject changed to the weather, and soon I found myself walking back to the store, feeling a bit of a klutz for having walked upon their pride some. I finished the baked potatoes, and then relaxed, lying back upon the sheep hides, only to have Francisco once again show up in the doorway with the third course; dessert. It looked like tapioca pudding, but upon tasting it I found that once again it was potatoes. Only this time with sugar added to make it sweeter.

Francisco stayed for a while, seemingly more at ease talking with me here alone than gathered with his family in his home. I don't really think they knew what to make of me and were rather shy because of it. Two completely different lifestyles meeting each other, two different cultures, but human beings nonetheless, interacting and making contact. It's a very healthy gesture and should be practiced more by all peoples.

After I had finished eating and Francisco left, I lay down on the sheep hides and found myself counting them as I fell asleep. I slept well, dreaming of herds of sheep foraging in potato fields, and woke up early, refreshed and ready for another day of hiking and probably the last. I didn't waste much time lounging around. I got up, washed up in a small stream that ran by the store, and ate a small breakfast of crackers and cheese from my pack. I thanked Francisco for his hospitality and left candy bars for his kids. Then, I walked down to the main trail that led out of town.

The sun was just coming up over the mountains as I passed through its shadow, walking out of town toward the Rio Chucpin Valley ten or more miles away. My destination was the town of Llumpa from where I planned to take the bus out of the Andes the next day. There weren't many people along this part of the trail, so the day was basically uneventful, that was until the trail broke through a small thicket and I found myself at the bottom of a *campesino's* fields.

As soon as I came into the open, I surprised a pack of dogs that were lying in the sun along the trail. They bolted, quickly scattering in all directions, while barking viciously. Soon they were buoyed by their own frenzy and began to circle me. They weren't large dogs. The biggest was a spaniel-mix, but since there were six of them, they were braver than usual. I stood still as they circled, hoping that the farmer up in the field would be able to call them off. Before he could get down there though, one lunged at me and bit my leg. That egged them on further, but I quickly left this passive role and gathered some large rocks, threatening them as I backed away down the trail. They snarled but saw that I meant business and didn't pursue me once I was out of their sight.

My first thought as I limped along the trail, cursing at my misfortune, was the possibility of having contracted rabies from that mutt's bite. There wasn't anything I could do about it since I was days away from any medical help. I consoled myself by figuring that the dogs acted out of fear rather than sickness.

The trail meandered around a hillside and brought into view a number of houses, sitting on a hog back, not more than a mile away. This had to be Llumpa, and I felt a little lighter on my feet knowing that the hike was nearly over.

CHAPTER 3:

LLUMPA, ANCASH, PERU – DAY 3

It was early afternoon when I walked into town, finding it pretty much closed for business, as are most Latin American towns at this time of day. I walked down one of the main streets of what seemed to be the center and found an open *tienda* where I bought an Inca Cola on ice. This one room shop also turned out to be

Matriarch of Llumpa

the ticket office for the bus. So, with ticket in hand, I felt a bit more secure as I walked around town, looking for a place to stay for the night. The bus was to leave the next morning at 9:00 a.m.

I wandered around town as people stared in wonder at this lone gringo in their midst. At one point I crossed a street, and an old woman, with a striking air of elegance about her accosted me and seemed to chastise me for being there. I couldn't understand her very well and tried, with little luck, to find out the source of her anger. She kept pointing her finger at me, saying "Gringo" over and over again, and looking at me disgustedly for having placed myself in front of her path. I felt confused and embarrassed, not sure what to do or say. I just smiled and walked up the street out of the way of her wrath.

The buildings along the street were made of thick, white-washed adobe, hiding courtyards and enclosures behind them. A passerby directed me to a doorway in the wall of one of these buildings. I walked through it into a small courtyard and looked around.

At the far end of the courtyard another old woman sat bundled up in a black, crocheted blanket. Eyes looking out at me from sockets that knew easier and younger days, she coughed, and acknowledged my presence with a grunted "*Hola, Gringo,*" and then quickly lost interest. I hesitated and then asked a little embarrassedly if her residence was a pension and she muttered that it was, at times. And then asked how many days did I plan to stay? "Just for the night," I said. "Where was the rest of the party?" "I am the party."

She tapped her cane on the floor and out from a dark room near her, a young girl came running, "Sí, abuela?" she said.

"La habitación de arriba, para el gringo." said the old woman. She turned, and for the first time smiled a little and asked if I wanted dinner. I replied that I would and asked for breakfast the next morning as well.

I got up and followed the girl across the muddy brick courtyard in the center of this four-walled fortress-like structure, passing a stone cistern in the middle of the grounds while stepping around dogs, dog shit, chickens, ducks and sheep. We then came to a set of wood stairs in one corner of the courtyard and climbed up to the top, where the girl pushed away bales of alfalfa and opened the double-doors into a large room with three beds. Two were just dirty mattresses, while the third had bedding that looked as if it had covered much flesh since last laundered.

I chose a fourth option of sleeping on top in my rented, bed-bug special sleeping bag.

The girl left, and I opened the wooden doors of the window that looked out onto the dirt street below. The sky looked as though the rains were an hour or two away, so I pulled out my rain and sweat-soaked clothes and hung them from the little balcony that projected out over the street. But I really didn't care if they dried or not.

I looked back up the street into the center of Llumpa and watched as two women sat next to a building spinning wool with their top-like spindles. They were busy with the telling of the afternoon news, which is every Andean woman's business while spinning. The top twirled on the ground with centrifugal force as the wool was wound with deft fingers that were in constant motion.

I came back inside and lay down for a needed rest that my body was crying out for. I slept for an hour and woke up not very refreshed because I kept smelling something rancid. I looked on the floor, seeing nothing, and then with the corner of my eye I caught a glimpse of a plastic chamber pot next to the far bed on the other side of the room. It was obvious from the smell and the sediment in the bottom that it hadn't been emptied in quite some time. I disgustedly picked up the pot and put it outside, leaving the doors open and then walked down the stairs to see about dinner.

The old woman still sat with her shawl wrapped around her in the small straight back chair. She looked very tired as she watched over the proceedings in the kitchen. The kitchen was in a hole in the wall with no light save that from the cooking fire in the middle of the dirt floor. I couldn't see inside, but by the clinking of forks and knives I figured that they must be eating. Then, a chubby, dirty-faced, barefoot little three-year old came out and sat down next to the entrance with a metal plate in his pudgy, little hands. His hands were very busy stuffing as much rice into his cheeks as a squirrel would, storing away for winter. He was healthy alright and didn't need to be asked if he wanted seconds.

I asked for a cup of tea, which was relayed by the old woman to the unseen cooks in the black hold of the kitchen. Sometime later, a hand reached out from the darkness into the twilight with a cup. The old woman took it and gave it to me in a way that seemed to hold no promise for a later cup. Or at least she hardly seemed to care for my thanks.

She seemed to notice my discomfort to her oblivious manner, as she felt obliged to tell me that she wasn't well. She complained of bronchitis but looked as if something worse might be more of a proper diagnosis. She couldn't sleep well, and her coughing seemed to pain her considerably. I felt for her and offered to give her some antibiotics from my drug supply. She declined since she was already taking penicillin with mixed results. She didn't seem to be very strong and might well be on the way to a worse time.

Her cane, however, kept busy punching at the starve-faced dogs that always gathered around the kitchen at this time. They tried to be as inconspicuous and friendly as possible but could never get past the wooden staff blocking their entrance to the kitchen and a piece of veal in the pudgy hands of a well-fed boy. They yelped as the cane jabbed them in the ribs and cowered from the wrath of an ever-watchful grandparent protecting the sanctity of the meal.

The twilight grew into darkness and finally they set a

table down away from the kitchen in a room inside the wall next to the street. The old woman, looking with tired eyes told me, *"Gringo, su comida es en el cuarto. Come usted, por favor. Gracias, senor."*

"Tengo mucho hambre, es verdad. Muchas gracias!" So, I walked out into the square and then turned into a room, flickering with candlelight. I sat at the end of a long table and ate as I thought of the days past and the days ahead and wondered how life was for these people.

Poverty, it seemed to me, was relative to the society in question as a whole. By our standards, much of the population of the Andes lived a life of substandard existence. Materially, this was true, but mentally I found them very much engrossed in living. They worked and played hard and smiled infectiously whenever our paths crossed. It is true that life is not easy and too often short for them, but they seemed to accept it that way and live day to day for the joy of just being.

I went to bed that night feeling healthy and stimulated from the last couple days hiking and looked forward to the bus ride back to Huaraz. I planned to spend a few more days with my friends at the Hostal Colomba, before leaving for Lima and a plane flight home. The next morning, I woke up early, 7:00 a.m., and lay in bed for a little while listening to a light rain tapping a natural rhythm on the balcony outside.

I was glad I wouldn't have to hike in it, as I looked out over the hills where rainclouds blanketed everything. I finally got up, packed my clothes, and climbed downstairs to the open courtyard. I went to say goodbye to the old woman, but she hadn't gotten up yet, although I could hear spasms of coughing in her room. Her daughter said that she would relay my wishes for a speedy recovery from her illness. I walked out through the door I had come through the night before and went off looking for the bus station.

Bus station? What bus station? There was none. Just a wide spot in the narrow, mountain road next to a tienda. So, I walked through Llumpa, waiting for the sound of diesel engines. I walked by a construction site where a group of men was building a rock wall and staircase. It ran up a hillside from a large house to the road above where I stood. The tools they used were all made of tree limbs with iron heads lashed to them. They used these for digging into the hill, and for splitting boulders into rock slabs for the stairs and spreading mortar. Even though their tools were simple, they worked at a steady pace, laying rock and mortar, accomplishing quite a lot even as I watched. They seemed to enjoy my curiosity, that is if smiles were any measure of their thoughts.

I walked on, after a while, leaving them to their labors and looked up the road toward the mountains. I could hear something up there rumbling like a diesel engine, and my eyes followed the snaking road until I spied something moving. It was a D8 caterpillar, blade down, pushing rocks into a small washout in the road. It was smoothing it over so the bus that was coming from Piscobamba, high up in the mountains, wouldn't have any trouble crossing over it. It was now 9:00 a.m. but still no sign of the bus. It wasn't until three hours later that the diesel engines finally could be heard coming down from the hills toward Llumpa. A lumbering, giant yellow hulk with black trim, it looked like an old Bluebird school bus converted into an overland hauler. I could well imagine, as I watched it pull into town, that it might be a rough ride to Huaraz. There wasn't anything about it that looked comfortable, except of course for the fact that it ran and would eventually get us out of the mountains.

I walked up to it and with ten or more people climbed aboard for what was supposed to be a short ride to the next town of San Luis, some 25 kilometers away. There were already about 15 people on the bus, along with some chickens and a couple of sheep. I was the only gringo in this busload of mountain people heading for the low hills to the west.

The bus driver was short, and in good shape. He looked like a man who took his responsibilities seriously but who also knew how to relax when the time was available. His chiseled face smiled easily and gregariously as he bantered with the passengers. Greasy, jet black hair lay long around his ears and was constantly being coaxed back from his face by an ever-present comb. By the number of young women hanging around the bus, this guy was obviously a real hit with the ladies. His name was Dionysius, which also happens to be the name of the Greek God of Wine. It seemed to fit him well, just by the personality that he projected.

After waiting twenty minutes or more, Dionysius started up the engines and headed down the road. I relaxed

Peruvian countryside

and looked out the window toward the hills that were on the other side of the Rio Chucpin, which we were paralleling a thousand feet above. We had been on the road for no more than fifteen minutes when we pulled around a curve and found ourselves face to face with a huge landslide. It had completely obliterated the road in front of us, leaving a 20-foot hill of dirt and rock in its place. I was stunned, thinking "Oh, shit! What the hell are we going to do now?"

The bus driver nonchalantly pulled over toward the cliff, parked the bus and got out telling everyone as he left that there would be a small delay until we could pass through. I took this to mean that the D8 would be here soon. There was no other way to move that hill. So, we all went outside and waited around for the caterpillar to show up and get us out of this impasse.

Dionysius sat on a rock looking down at the black Rio Chucpin a thousand feet below. His radio blared *Saturday Night Fever,* while raindrops pounded a steady percussion to the disco beat. A foreboding was creeping into my psyche as I watched the swollen river, black as night, cutting a swath through the saturated hills. I got up from the cliff's edge and walked over to the bus, deciding to sit out of the rain for a while. The people on the bus were lounging around, seemingly oblivious to any of the anxiety that I was feeling. I guess it probably had something to do with the fact that they were from here, and I wasn't. The only gringo on the bus, I didn't know that my premonitions would be realized before anyone could imagine.

After about an hour, the D8 caterpillar lumbered its way down the road to us. The driver hardly blinked as he drove the earth mover up to the gigantic mudslide. The landslide was no match for this gargantuan hunk of steel on movable tracks. It had no problem in getting rid of the dirt. The cat just pushed it over the edge to the river below. I thought to myself, "Man, these guys have got guts." The driver went right out to the edge of the slope with the blade hanging out over the cliff, only a hair from oblivion. Within another half an hour he had managed to reduce this 20-foot hill into level ground. As soon as he backed out of the way, we all boarded the bus again, and Dionysius drove on through the muck. As he drove, the rear end slid sideways toward the edge and I found myself looking into the hands of God, which were waiting to carry us away if we moved a few inches more. I looked across the aisle and seriously contemplated jumping out the half-opened window. As luck would have it, we were out of the mud just when it seemed that all was lost. I thought then that what we had just gone through had to be the worst road conditions that we would ever encounter. I was proved wrong as the day progressed.

Road to San Luis

The road itself descended in a meandering course along a steep precipice, eventually ending up at the river below. The road was never wider than fifteen feet and so narrow in some places that the bus could barely fit. Those narrow places could stretch for a half mile or more. What was worse was that now, during the rainy season, conditions changed minute by minute, as rocks and boulders often rolled off the banks above us and onto the road in front.

Not more than half a mile beyond the mudslide, we began encountering rocks on the road. Since it was too narrow to go around them, the apprentice drivers that were training with Dionysius got off and began rolling them over the edge of the cliff. When we came to another huge rock slide, I thought to myself, "What the hell have I gotten myself into?" Dionysius turned, facing the passengers, telling us we had no choice but to get picks and shovels and dig the road out by hand. I hoped that I had misunderstood his Spanish, but I found myself, with the other men, outside facing a rockslide, some three or four feet deep and 20 or more feet in breadth. The picks and shovels consisted of one pick with a broken handle and two shovels. So, we had to roll the boulders over the cliff mostly by hand.

It seemed like an impossible task, but somehow, we managed to roll the biggest boulders and were then able to level out a path over which the driver could maneuver the

"Condor de Chavín" to safety.

Dionysius sent everyone to the other side of the rock slide and then started the bus. He moved the front tires up onto the slide. The front end reared up and tilted from side to side as the tires went from one rock to another, but the rear end had a powerful drive train and soon he made it across, and we all piled back in. The distance that we naturally felt amongst each other was soon giving over to a camaraderie for the mutual dangers that we faced. For some reason, I once again felt that our path was open now, and we would soon be in San Luis.

As soon as I relaxed, we came around a corner and found ourselves with an even worse predicament than any of the previous ones. It seems that a small drainage had been dumping water onto the road from the embankment above. This had managed to cut the road back from the cliff to where it was not wide enough for the bus to make it through. With the bus being eight feet wide and road cut back to seven feet, I knew that my pack would once again be on my back and my feet would be my transportation. Dionysius, who seemingly was not intimidated by anything, had other ideas.

He immediately got out the pick and shovels and once again ordered the men off the bus. He figured that we could dig into the hillside and build a road. I couldn't believe he was serious. Needless to say, he was. His plan was to dig out a notch into the hillside far enough so that he could poke the front end of the bus into it, and then turn a hard left, carving the left front tire around the slice in the road. "What about the rear end?" I thought. It all seemed totally ludicrous, but what choice did we have? He was the one taking all the chances. So, dig we did, and after an hour or so we had dug out a notch about two feet into the hillside and five feet wide. It was maybe wide enough to pull the front end into but still I couldn't see how the rear end could make it. Besides, even if he did make it through, he still had a hundred yards of pure muck on the other side to negotiate. Again, there was the distinct prospect of sliding off the road and over the cliff.

Dionysius got back on the bus, telling everyone to go to the other side past the mudslide while he drove through. His face had a look of determination, and the muscles in his neck were taut with the anticipation of another razor's edge to walk along. It was always he alone, with his bus, pitting himself against death and destruction if he were to miscalculate. Life was dealt with from day to day on a level of high intensity. To the apprentices that rode with him, he was the epitome of the Macho man. They would go anywhere with him, knowing that theirs was the way of true men. They received no pay, but when the road conditions were right, one of them would drive the bus while Dionysius slept. And for Dionysius's part, he treated them as young friends and future colleagues.

He started up the bus, and with diesel engines chugging, pushed the nose into the notch cut out of the embankment. The left front wheel grazed the edge of the cliff as the right front closed in on the hill. Then with a hard-left turn, he carved around the wedge of nothingness that had sliced into the road, and he poured on the diesel. The back tires responded with a roar, grinding dirt out from under them. I could see that the left rear tire was going to go over the cliff, and my heart seemed to stop when it came to the edge. It went over the crevasse, the bus tipped to the left, but the right wheel still grabbed, and the momentum pulled the left wheel back up onto the road and immediately onto the mudslide in front. Again, the bus swayed from side to side as it pushed through the muck, edging closer and closer to the precipice that looked down over the Rio Chucpin below. As before, the tires reached the edge and miraculously floated back a few feet toward the middle of the road. Finally, the bus reached dry ground on the other side. Another obstacle, another trial, another moment in the life of an Andean bus driver. Amen.

Rio Chucpin at flood stage

This last display of courage and insanity brought a lot of hugs and screams from the passengers. I guess they finally decided that this last circus event was a little out of the ordinary. For me, I was practically a nervous wreck. I mean, "How the hell did I get into this mess in the first place?" As it turns out, I could have walked as fast as it

took us to get to where we were and with a lot less trauma!
A thought crossed my mind that maybe I should do just
that: get my pack and get out while the getting was good.
After a few moments of reflection, allowing my heart to
lower its pace to a more normal rate, I thought otherwise. I
had gone this far with the bus, and we should be more than
halfway to San Luis by now. Besides, what more could
happen? We were getting close to the bottom of the
canyon, and once we crossed the Rio Chucpin, San Luis
was but a few miles away. No more problems! Ignorance is
bliss, especially for those as naïve as myself.

I got back on the bus and moved back to my seat in the
rear. Dionysius put it in gear and we again chugged
forward, anticipating a clear road. At least, I did. Sitting
there in this long Bluebird, my eyes wandered around the
bus picking up what my senses could pack into my brain.

The sounds were that of people talking, a couple of
babies crying, until mothers' breasts pacified their anger.
Chickens, with legs tied and placed in burlap sacks, were
rustling inside their cocoons, protesting the undignified
position they had been placed in. Little did they know that
they were headed for market and the butcher's razor-sharp

blade that would end their protests, once and for all. My lack of sympathy for them was dictated by the incessant racket that they seemed to make, especially when I started to doze off. The smells were pungent, as they would be with a bus full of mountain people and some of their livestock. Smells of manure mixed with diesel permeated the sweaty atmosphere inside, necessitating the open windows. Actually, I didn't mind. I'm sure the odor coming from me was no better or worse than anyone else, especially since I hadn't had a bath in ten days of travel.

My eyes wandered from the bus to the scene outside. We were now near the bottom of the river canyon. Looking out, I could see by the hills around us why we were having so much trouble with the roads. There were no trees. Only short grass, and there was no way that erosion could be stopped. Since nothing stopped the water, it's no wonder that mudslides and rocks were a common problem on these roads.

I realized, more than ever, that what we had gone through was routine for the Andes Mountains. In fact, the situation changed from day to day, as new slides developed, and more formidable obstacles were placed in front to test these, "Knights of the Andes." What a job: putting your life on the line every time you entered the, 'Jaws of the Condor' as it were. But these people depended on the roads for communication and supplies. No matter what, they had to be kept open, despite any obstacles. At least, it was certainly treated like this by the bus drivers.

I looked ahead, and up the river canyon, I saw the buildings of San Luis about five miles across the gorge. We had been on the bus now for eight hours and I was ready for a beer and something to eat. By the looks of it, we would be there in thirty minutes or so. Maybe less! With this in mind, I relaxed more, realizing that all was smooth sailing from here out.

We came to the bottom of the gorge and looked upon the black churning foam of a river gone mad. The roar was deafening, like standing at the bottom of Angel Falls in Venezuela. The water rushed past, moving with a speed and force that only a system of dams, like the ones on the Columbia River, would be able to control. Here in these mountains, it was a force that was uncontrollable and all powerful. Humbly we approached the concrete bridge that straddled the 100-yard torrent. As we crossed, I looked down and felt a certain exhilaration that comes from seeing something that is totally free and untamed.

On the other side, we immediately started to climb, zig-zagging our way up the hill. The road seemed to be wider here, and I was glad to see that there weren't any rocks on it. We reached a point a few hundred feet above the river, and then we started going more directly south, along the hillside toward San Luis. We had traveled about a mile and a half, when we came around a corner and started to climb again, only to find that the road ahead had been completely obliterated.

Cliffs of crumbling rock on either side of the road had fallen in and completely blocked our path. It felt like something out of Ulysses. I was just waiting for a giant cyclops to appear with a huge boulder held over his head to dash us into oblivion. This really did look scary. Mainly because at any moment the cliffs could crumble even further sending rocks crashing down on the road, just as we were trying to dig a path for the bus. And those rocks were at least fifty feet above us, and seemed very brittle, just waiting for any vibration to jar them loose. I didn't like the looks of the whole thing, but I guess there wasn't a choice.

I could have walked out, I guess, but I didn't feel like deserting these people, especially after all the trials we had been through to get here. So again, we all got out of the bus and moved toward the rock hill in front of us. The procedure was to try and clear a path, wide enough for the bus to go through. Since it was impossible to move all the rocks, we moved the biggest, and tried to level a path with the smaller boulders. I was working on one side of the road, when a friend softly called to me, *"Gringo, arriba,"* he said. I looked above me and there, perched precariously on a small outcrop, was a giant boulder, just ready to drop anytime. I quietly put down whatever rock I had picked up and moved out from underneath the deadly shadow of my would-be assassin.

Coming up to the apex of the hill, we approached a boulder in the middle of the path that was going to pose a problem. It was four feet in diameter and solid. There wasn't any way we could budge it by pushing, so another solution was needed.

Dionysius looked up to the side of the road and spied a tree that had been pulled from the ground by the slide. It was about six inches in diameter, and twenty feet long. So, we got eight men on it and braced it under the rock as far as we could get with a rock underneath for leverage. Putting all our weight into it, the tree bent way over, but slowly it budged the boulder over a foot. It worked! A few more efforts like that, and it was pushed out of the way far enough to allow the bus to pass.

Dionysius walked back down the hill to the bus, and the rest of us walked to the top. He had a couple of hundred yards of crumbling rock to avoid disturbing. We watched as he started the engines and once again approached a bed of boulders, his front tires rearing up onto the slide, not unlike a horse. The powerful drive train kept pushing, and finally, the whole bus was up, tipping from side to side, as it went from boulder to boulder. It wasn't long before he came to the top of the hill and the safety of the road on the other side. Again, we all boarded the bus, and "headed on down the highway."

We travelled for a mile or two when Dionysius suddenly pulled over to the side of the road. He motioned for the men to get up and follow him out. I wondered what the problem could be now. We headed over the side of the road, down to where a small thatch-roofed hut sat on the hillside. A man stood waiting there for us, as Dionysius held his arms out and embraced him, as good Latin friends are accustomed to doing. The man then opened a cellar door beside him and went inside. He returned, carrying what looked like a pottery crock. Opening it up, he took a gourd that was cut in half, and dipped out a yellowish liquid, giving it to Dionysius. Taking a long pull from the gourd, he then passed it to the rest of us. I hoped it wasn't water and took a sip. Hmm, not bad! It had an effervescence to it and was most assuredly alcoholic. It turned out to be beer, fermented from corn, called *'chicha.'* We all had numerous swigs, quenching the nagging thirsts that had developed from building roads all day. After what we had been through, this was an appropriate reward for all our efforts.

Finally, we grudgingly relinquished the gourd to our new-found friend and walked back up the hill to the road. I had a glow on and felt really healthy and content with the camaraderie of my *campesino* friends. These were the ordinary people of the Andes. The peasants who tilled the soil for the rich landlords who lived in the expensive and expansive haciendas. For me, these were the real people of the Andes.

The bus started up again, and we traveled along another ridge. The road was narrow, probably twelve feet wide, but I knew that San Luis was only about one mile away. Relaxed and thinking about fried chicken, steak or anything that would fill the hole in my stomach, I looked ahead. To my delight, about a half a mile as the crow flies, I saw the white buildings of the village. They looked inviting, offering shelter and peace in a world of malevolent forces. We rounded a curve, not more than half a mile from town, where once again, we found ourselves face to face with an obstacle of seemingly impossible odds.

A small creek, turned into a raging torrent, had flashed over the hill above and had dug a bed in the road. Water was pouring out of the hillside, slashing through the road and crashing down to the river a few hundred feet below. On both sides of this small gorge lay huge mudslides that once again wiped out the road. There was a collective hush within the bus. We all gaped at the worst problem we had come across during a day of Murphy's Law come true.

Dionysius stopped the bus at the mudslide, and dazedly, we all filtered out. We walked over to the edge of the small gorge and watched the torrent where the road used to be. The water had cut a swath twenty feet wide and what looked to be four feet deep. But it was really hard to tell, because we couldn't see the bottom where the water crashed from the hill above. What to do?

It didn't look like there was much we could do, actually. Even if Dionysius could have negotiated the mudslide, which angled precariously to the edge of the cliff from a high spot at the base of the hill, he would still have to face a swollen creek. To my amazement he laid out plans to do just that. He got us all to work trying to implement them. To me, it seemed totally fruitless. How could any negative arguments have any effect on one as hell-bent and bull-headed as that guy? The plan was to pull the biggest rocks out of the slide and throw them into the water, trying to build up a bridge for the bus to cross.

The job was frustrating, since there was so much mud it was hard to find rocks to pull out. When we did, they just sank out of sight when we threw them into a seemingly bottomless torrent. Dionysius also instructed us to throw dry dirt on the edge of both sides of the gorge, in case the back tires needed traction. So, a few stayed on one side while three or four men, including myself, walked through the water, holding onto each other, fighting the swift current pushing against us. It was difficult finding dry dirt because of all the mud, but we managed and spread it along the edge of the gorge and especially heavy at the edge of the cliff. Just in case.

By the looks of it, we had hardly made a dent in the slides and couldn't see how the bus could possibly make it. First of all, the mudslide was at an acute angle from the hill to the cliff. Even if the bus could get moving on it, the possibility of it rolling over the cliff was very real. Even if it were possible to make it to the gorge, it then had to drop down into the water at a steep angle by which the front end might be completely immersed. While I was thinking of all these disastrous scenarios, Dionysius was starting the engine.

All eyes and prayers were focused upon this man and his machine tempting fate, as usual. He moved the bus up as close to the hillside as he could get and walked the front end up onto the slide. He didn't seem to be at too dangerous an angle until he got the back tires into it. He tipped at such an angle that it looked like he would roll at any second. His saving grace was that he kept the momentum up, and by the time it looked like it was all over, he was at the edge of the gorge. Continuing to move, for fear of flipping, he pushed the front down into the torrential water, while the back end almost stood up behind it, the angle was so steep. The water crashed against the front of the bus, rushing up the bottom of the windshield. At least it didn't go over the top of the bus as I had feared. The rear end came down off the slide and now the whole bus was in. The water here came up past the bumper which made it about four feet deep. Not real deep compared to the bus but coming at such a force that it pushed the bus toward the edge of the cliff, all the while the back tires spun, trying to gain traction on the rocks at the bottom. Slowly, ever so slowly, he made progress and managed to get the front tires up onto the slide on the other side. The back tires were only a few feet from the edge of the cliff, as he pulled the back end up to the slide. He moved the left rear tire up on the slide, but it started to spin again. The water all the while slammed against the bus. He couldn't get any traction at all and the right rear tire was inches from going over the cliff.

Just when it seemed like he was gone to the river below, the left rear tire found a purchase on the dry dirt that we had amassed at the edge of the cliff, and it pulled the other tire up onto the other side, avoiding a 500-foot drop into oblivion. Everyone yelled and screamed. Women cried. Men slapped each other on the backs, and we all mobbed Dionysius as he came out of the bus, smiling triumphantly.

To say that Dionysius was a hero in the eyes of everyone, and not just to his young apprentices, was pretty accurate. Considering what he had brought us through in the last twelve hours, I guess he had reason to feel a little cocky. To think that he had to face similar obstacles each trip into these mountains made one realize how short life can be. I wouldn't have traded places with him for anything.

Sam Woolsey

CHAPTER 4:

SAN LUIS, ANCASH, PERU – DAY 4

Linda and Victoria at Restorante San Luis

Buxom and tall, Linda was a young woman with whom conversation was a pleasure, even though I couldn't speak her language, nor she mine.   Actually,   our imagination and the little Spanish I did know managed to convey the message I was trying to get across. Her sister, Victoria, another flatteringly beautiful woman, watched quietly and listened intently as we talked animatedly. She was a little shorter than Linda, with long raven-black hair, and also generously endowed. With these two lovely ladies, I passed a very enjoyable evening, laughing, drinking and carrying on until their mother, the proprietress, came to tell us it was time to close up, and go home. I was immediately deflated, since I had hoped somehow to wear the evening long with one of these two temptresses. Even worse, I had the vision of having to sleep on the bus, with a bunch of snoring *campesino*s, clucking chickens, and a restless sheep or two.

To my surprise, Linda took me by the hand and led me out of the restaurant and into the moonlit street. I didn't say anything, letting her choose whatever path that she willed, just as long as it was away from the restaurant and the bus. Walking down the deserted street, we passed beneath street lights that seemed to be just lanterns, tied to the tops of wooden poles. I felt as if I had been dropped into an old western town of south Colorado in the 1800's. It was the kind of place "Butch and Sundance" would have recognized.

After a couple of blocks, we came to the bottom of the dirt street and found ourselves in front of a large, two story adobe building. We opened a wooden door and stepped from the street into a courtyard protected by walls on four sides. This was her parents' home and they were obviously well off.

I found out later that her father was an agriculture professor who worked with the Indians in the mountains of the Cordillera Blanca. He was hardly ever at home, as was the case then. She told me she was a law student in Lima, while her sister, Victoria, was a medical student there.

I picked right up on that and told her that I was Robert Redford and was down here doing research for a movie on the Amazons of the Western Amazon. She looked at me dumbfounded for a second and then we both burst into laughter. She looked at me again, shaking her head, and then pointed to the room upstairs. She told me there was a cot set up for me there. I was grateful to her but was disappointed that I would be sleeping alone. I'll bet that never happened to Bob Redford!

I climbed the ladder and found a dark room at the top, save for a slit of moonlight coming through a crack in a small door that opened out onto the village below. I groped for a bed, blindly feeling in the dark, and just about jumped out of my shoes when I put my hand on something that moved. I backed up and opened the door to the window

Victoria, Sam, Linda and Nancy

above the street, and let the moonlight bathe the scene in front of me. I wasn't the only one here. The room had six cots and five of them were occupied. I couldn't understand why I hadn't heard them upon entering the room. Standing there, I realized that not one moved, snored, or even

breathed hard. Spooked, I lay down on the empty cot and
went to sleep.

Sometime later in the evening, I heard a commotion
going on downstairs out on the street. Somebody, or some
bodies were pounding on a door of this adobe villa. They
were loudly, drunkenly, beseeching the occupants inside to
let them in. Inside, a man yelled at them, which didn't seem
to dampen their spirits, as they continued to bang on the
door. I then realized that their enthusiasm was dictated by
the pouring rain that had taken the place of the earlier
moonlight. After about fifteen minutes of this exchange
between outside and inside, everything became quiet once
again. I gratefully let my mind drift back into
unconsciousness. After a while, my dreams began to take
on a melodic turn, and I realized as I awoke that reality was
invading slumber once again. Only this time the noises
were from three voices and at least two guitars beautifully
harmonizing a serenade to the holder of the key, inside the
villa. I lay there and let the harmony of their tenor, bass and
baritone voices lull me along. After another fifteen minutes
or more of this, I heard voices downstairs and a door
opened whereby the three *caballeros* were allowed sanctuary

from the rains. I smiled to myself, thinking of how very Latin that whole exchange had been.

The next morning, I awoke to find that everyone else in the room had gotten up and was heading down the stairs. I drifted back to sleep for a little while longer, then decided I had better get up and see what was happening with the bus. I threw on my clothes and climbed down the ladder into the courtyard. At the bottom I investigated a small alcove off the courtyard. There on a cot made for one and a half, lay the three *caballeros*, covered with their coats. One of them looked out as I passed by, smiling with the weak pain of a bad hangover. I thanked him for the serenade the night before, and he just smiled, raising his hand in greeting.

The rains had stopped, but the ground was saturated, as water flowed wherever a low spot was located. A pit in my stomach developed, as anxiety tried to slip in and influence my mood. Dionysius had gotten us this far through this rain-swollen country; I couldn't imagine him quitting now.

I walked along mud-slogged streets to the restaurant with blue skies and an early sun holding out a promise of dry weather, for at least a few hours. The bus was sitting next to the wall of the restaurant, and heads were poking out as I came up. It was 9:00 a.m. and they were all awake and getting anxious to leave. I asked where Dionysius was, and they pointed to the restaurant. I went inside, lowering my head as I went through the door. I swear every doorway in these villages was no more than 5'11" high, which is a pain when you are six feet or taller. Abdul Jabbar would never survive down here!

I found Dionysius sitting at a large table in a room off the street. Sitting with him were two other men. They both wore uniforms and had pistols strapped to their hips. The local constable and his deputy, I presumed. As they sat there another fellow came in and Dionysius got up and gave him a bear hug. They all sat down and before long two or three more guys showed up and so did liters of cold beer from the cooler. I sat in the kitchen adjacent to the large dining room and ate breakfast while talking with Linda and Victoria. Occasionally, my curiosity would get the better of me and I'd stick my head around the corner and see what the drinking buddies were up to. I gathered by the number of empty bottles on the table that everyone was sufficiently primed for action. Any kind of action would do.

And so, it was that Linda, catering to their sudsy needs, found herself the focus of attention, especially when she brought another armload of ice cold brew. She had no problems, since these guys were more interested in drinking and talking than chasing her around a table. I think I would have chosen the latter option myself.

Around noon I began to get a little concerned that the *compañeros* were maybe carrying this all a bit too far. Especially since everyone was on the bus waiting for Dionysius to start it up and head down the road. But as I stuck my head in the room to see what was happening, Dionysius saw me and yelled out, *"Roberto, Robert, ¡Venga aqui!* I thought to myself, Robert Redford is now well known in San Luis. I had no choice but to join in now as otherwise it would be an insult to Dionysius. I had no desire to cause any problems with him. I sat down at the long table between Dionysius and the Chief of Police.

There had to have been a dozen full bottles on the table and twice as many empty. But I noticed right off that there was only one glass between six people. I quickly discovered why. Latin men always drink out of the same glass when partying like this. One man will fill the glass, raise it in salutation to his *amigos* and drink it down in one gulp, afterwards shaking what is left in the glass out onto the floor. And then he passes the bottle and glass to the next man on his right. In a public place like this, women don't usually get involved. Although in private, they join occasionally.

Dionysius introduced everyone around the table to me and then passed me the glass. I performed the required ritual, throwing the foam on the floor and passed the bottle and glass then to him. I was the focal point of attention for a while, but they found that my command of Spanish was good only for simple conversation and quickly grew disinterested, which was fine with me. A while later, Dionysius got up with three or four other guys and went out in the sunlight for some fresh air. That left me there alone, except for a guy across from me who was drunkenly staring at me with a weird smirk on his face. I ignored him at first, but then started to get kind of annoyed, so I looked at him intently also, waiting to see what he would do.

Well, what he did surprised me. He leaned over the

table, all the while looking at me and swept a finger across his throat and began jabbering about the military and gringos. I couldn't really understand him, since he was drunk, and his speech slurred, but he seemed to be politically motivated in his conversation. And if that didn't get my attention, then the knife that he pulled out from under the table definitely did. It was narrow and long, the kind of knife for sticking somebody with. I pretended to ignore it and the fact that he was making a point to me of how sharp it was. I thought to myself, " Whatever I do, I can't let this guy think he's got me buffaloed." He went on fingering his blade and brought his finger across his throat a few more times to emphasize his dislike for authority and gringos, not necessarily in that order.

In my broken Spanish, I asked him if he was a follower of Che Guevara, the late Cuban revolutionary. He smiled and asked how I knew of the great man. I told him I couldn't help but know of him, especially up here in the mountains, where his picture was everywhere, even on the mud flaps of diesel trucks. We both laughed at this one, and the air seemed to lighten up a little. It wasn't long before the two cops and Dionysius came weaving back inside. The sometime guerrilla put his blade away, but from the looks of things, the police could care less. From what I gathered by all of this, it didn't matter what political party was in power. Up here in the mountains, where the law was diluted so far from its source in Lima, people thought and did just what they pleased. To many people Che Guevara was a hero, who had honestly tried to better the plight of the common *campesino*.

In San Luis, the right-wing police and my guerrilla friend drank toasts to each other, until at some other time intangible forces produced the right mixture which would have them at each other's throats. In the Andes that sort of situation could happen at any time. In the Peruvian Andes, as in Guatemala, where the population is primarily poor Indians, and the rich Spanish-mix own the lands, unrest is only a bad crop away.

Once everyone was back inside and settled at the table, the party resumed. After two hours of drinking like this, I found my head continually creeping toward the table, and I realized this wasn't a very comfortable place to sleep. I begged off any more beer, thanking my *compañeros* for the good time, and weaved a path to the bus where I joined the people and chickens for an early afternoon nap.

I woke up a couple of hours later and found almost everyone in the bus. It was almost 4:00 p.m. and we were supposed to have left for Huaraz by 1:00 p.m. Some of them asked me if I knew when we were going. I told them I had no idea, as my head continued to swim in a sea of beer. I laid back down for a minute, and soon decided I had better see what happened to Dionysius. I got up and

Condor de Chavín outside Restorante San Luis

stepped out into the street, just as the Chief of Police and his deputy came staggering out of the restaurant. Both held onto each other tightly, to prevent either from falling over. They weaved a path to the police station and covered three or four times more ground than the journey would take normally. If there had been any traffic on that street, they would have been run over by oncoming and outgoing.

I walked into the restaurant, and there among at least thirty empty bottles of beer sat the lone *caballero*. His head was almost touching his chest. He looked up at me with glazed and swimming eyes and sputtered out a greeting, "Hola, Roberto!" I thought to myself, "This is hopeless, he'll never be able to drive now." I looked at him sitting there pie-eyed and told him that I was worried that he wouldn't be able to drive us out of there today. Dionysius looked up at me and with his eyes apologized profusely. He didn't want me to be disappointed in him, especially since I was a foreigner. Then to my surprise, he somehow stood up and walked on his own power back into the kitchen. I followed a few minutes later and this is what I found:

Dionysius shook his head, feeling the blood
flow once again to his temples as he focused upon
a sober world, with eyes drunken and blotched.
For any other man this would be the scene the

morning after an all-night binge, but for our hero, it was the result of a five-minute head massage from water pumped over the back of his head from a well, after an all-day binge.

I watched him as he stood there, not sure what his next move would be. No problem. He knew what came next. He walked out through the slop and opened the gate where the pigs and cows were lounging. He was out there for what seemed to be a good twenty minutes. I got a little worried that maybe one of the four hundred-pound sows might have decided to attack him for the foul smell he exuded. Just when I thought to make mention of it to Victoria and Linda, here he returned in all his glory. Face fresh, comb out laying back the grease of his thick, black hair. He looked as if he had just gotten up from a twelve-hour sleep and was ready to fight any mad bull that dared to snort and paw in front of his path. He sat down, ordered a large mug of coffee, steak and eggs, and proceeded to fill his belly with a passion, all the while talking expansively to the beauties who served him. He winked at them and pinched their butts as they turned from the table to tend to the grill. The girls squealed, protesting, which brought roars from Dionysius's steak-packed cheeks.

Dionysius and Amigos at Restorante San Luis

If there was ever a working model of machismo, I have no doubt that he would have felt that he fit the mold and then broke it. I have never seen a more radical transformation from drunk to sober and probably never will! True there was plenty of alcohol still running through his system, but he had it handled and under control.

After he had eaten, we got up and went outside to where the bus sat next to the restaurant on the road. There was a problem developing, as we stood there looking at the street in front of the bus. I had known that it was there since we arrived in this little town, but for some reason it didn't register as something we would have to deal with.

The street ahead ran for two blocks with a side street dividing it. It was sixteen feet wide with buildings on both sides. The first block was level, but the second block was a steep hill that was muddy and slick from the constant rains. That wasn't the whole problem. The main dilemma was that a water system was being put in and workers had dug a deep ditch practically down the middle of the blocks, leaving only the side street open to traffic.

Basically, what this meant was that there wasn't room for a bus to get out of town. Until they had fixed the road, that is, and who knew when that might be. The thought of this panicked me a little. Don't get me wrong, I would have loved to stay and spend time with Linda and Victoria, but I had a plane to catch from Lima. A charter plane no less, and I was just about out of money, so I didn't want to miss it.

Dionysius stood in the street talking with what turned out to be a fellow bus driver, who had just come from Huaraz. My mood picked up as it dawned on me that this guy got here, so there must be a way out of town after all. There was a difference however, his bus was at least five feet shorter and narrower. Ours was about the size of a long school bus. Also, to get into town, he came downhill, while we were going the opposite direction. As it turned out, he had enough room to pass between the ditch and mortared wall on the block which was the hill, but for our bus to retrace his steps and go uphill through all the muck seemed, again, nearly impossible. First, there would be no way to do it except with a run at it, which was rough, because the only way to get to it was by the side street that divided the two blocks. That side street was bordered by high adobe buildings until it came to the intersection. It would be difficult for a car, but for a long bus the notion of screaming down a side street at forty miles per hour or better, and then negotiating a 90°turn, to head up a steep strip of road twelve feet wide between a ditch and a wall seemed ludicrous. It would have to be perfect in all ways, and there was still no guarantee that the bus could keep from spinning out of control the fifty yards to the top of the hill.

All these scenarios flashed through my mind, as once again Dionysius got everyone off the bus to hike the two blocks up to the top of the hill. The passengers of the bus and all the townspeople stood there, waiting for the action that was about to happen. The road here was muddy, with a small stream running down from the top, keeping it well lubricated. Dionysius would be forced to come up a narrow chute, between a mortared wall and the ditch, along a twelve-foot-wide strip which at the very top was the steepest and turn a corner at almost ninety degrees.

With this in mind, we all waited for the sound of an engine. It wasn't long before our wish was granted. A dull roar could be heard coming out and up from the buildings that bordered the side street that he had to race down. The roar soon became an all-pervading sound that seemed to come from everywhere. I knew he was going fast, as fast as he could. He would have to. That was for certain. The roar turned into a blast, and out from between the left corner buildings the bus flew. Just as the back end hit the open air, Dionysius turned the front end ninety degrees, swinging that back end around in almost mid-air, back tires spinning with all of the RPM's the bus could muster. The wheels hit the ground, digging into the dirt and shot the bus up the road like a sling shot.

Dionysius had the bus pointed in just the right direction

as it came roaring up the hill, making it to the very top until the steepest point where it turned the corner. The back tires began to spin, getting no traction so that the bus started sliding backwards out of control. The back tires kept spinning, while the bus kept sliding. Frantically, the boys who worked for Dioysius moved large rocks in the path of the back tires, risking their necks to get the bus stopped before it went into the ditch or plowed into the stone wall on the other side. The tires hit the rocks, but the momentum carried them up and over. Then the back end slid into the stone wall, knocking off three or four feet from the top. This slowed it down and rocks were placed behind the back tires, which finally brought the bus to a stop. There the bus sat, steam rising from the tires that had run some hard, fast miles, but never gaining more than a hundred feet of ground. Another thirty feet and he would have been over the top. Not this time, and probably not next time. Especially considering how slick the road was and the steepness of the hill.

We all stood around looking at the bus sitting with the rear end up against the wall, and a small stream of water running underneath. There seemed to be a collective hush for a minute as we all wondered how Dionysius would pull this one off.

As the men of the bus began working around it, I snapped to, and found myself in there also. We were trying to locate dry dirt to place in front of the wheels, so they would have some traction. That was a difficult task, since everything seemed to be wet. We put down as much as we could find, and then Dionysius signaled that he was ready to try it again. He revved up the engine until it was almost whining, and then popped the clutch. The back tires lurched forward from the protection of the rocks behind them hitting the dry dirt and gaining some traction, but as soon as the front end reached the steep corner at the top of the hill, the back tires began spinning again. Falling backward, the bus slid, grazing the wall again, knocking stones down off the top of it. This slowed the bus a little, but then it began sliding faster and closer to the ditch on the other side. The young men again ran toward the moving wheels with large rocks, but the bus just went up and over the tops of them, coming back down with a crash, and continued down the hill. Again, they ran behind the wheels with more boulders, and with this effort the bus climbed up on top of the rocks and stayed there, perched precariously a foot above the road.

Dionysius jumped out of the bus and told us all to get as much dry dirt as possible and put it under the wheels. Well, I want to tell you I didn't like that idea at all, because those rocks could slip out from under the tires at any time. There was nothing else to be done. So, we all searched high and low for dry dirt, finding it only by the hands full. We put much of the dirt, mixed with some gravel, directly under the wheels so that when they hit the ground, they would have good traction right at the start. We then piled more dirt in a line between the front and rear tires. As soon as we had done this, the constant stream of water coming down the hill was eating away at it again.

Dionysius jumped back into the driver's seat and revved up the motor. He popped the clutch and the back tires flew off the rocks, landing on the dry dirt with a tremendous crash. The rear end almost touched the ground. With this jolt the Condor of Chavín leapt forward and stayed on the line of dry dirt for another fifteen feet, gaining some momentum. The front end hit the steep corner again, but this time the back tires didn't start to spin until the whole bus was almost on top and around the corner. The momentum now was still going forward. As the tires spun, they kept going ahead, finally squirming and sliding to the level ground on top.

At this the crowd let out a collective roar, and quickly gathered around the bus to slap Dionysius on the back for a very entertaining feat of daring. He was one big smile from ear to ear. He loved this kind of treatment, and I didn't blame him. I had to admit, the guy was not one to back away from anything that life had to dish out. The more difficult, the better. The worse the odds, the greater the challenge. He was only 5'6", but all guts. I don't know what the life expectancy of an Andes bus driver is, but it's got to be short. I have no doubt that he'll beat those odds also.

Dionysius didn't revel in this adulation for long and was soon back on the bus, blasting the horn for all the passengers to return. I had been talking with Linda and Victoria, wistfully fantasizing to myself about staying for a while. But, I was broke, or almost, had a plane to catch in a few days, and was kind of anxious to leave.

We said our goodbyes, promising to write. Once again, I

boarded the bus, anticipating an easy road ahead, and except for the remnants of a flash flood that had turned the road into a dry river bed, we had no problems. In fact, after what we had been through, my reaction to anything more was rather jaded. I sat in the back of the bus, letting my mind drift as we continued along through the treeless hills expecting to reach the main north-south highway within another twelve hours.

My peace was occasionally broken by the crying of a small child in the seat in front of me. He actually wasn't too bad, but it was more the nosiness of his young father that was annoying. The father also happened to be a federal policeman. I remembered him as being the one male who wouldn't get his hands dirty to try and help get the bus up to the top of the hill. He carried an air of self-importance that obnoxiously wore on me. He wanted to know who I was, where I was from, what the purpose of my visit was, etc. etc. I told him whatever lies came to the top of my head.

His interest wasn't lost upon the other people of the bus either. They snickered and poked fun at me with their eyes for the unwanted company I was keeping. For them, he represented an outside annoyance that was the federal government with all its arrogance, self-importance, and above it all, attitude. For him, the *campesinos* were ignorant peasants who needed to be kept under foot. So, by dealing with me, he fashioned a self-importance that hopefully would impress the other passengers. Of course, the people weren't blind to his machinations which caused the snickering and discreet smiles. It just brought me back to the reality that I was a gringo, and would always be one, no matter how long I might have remained there.

I lay back in my seat pretending to sleep. Soon the cop became bored with me and returned his attention to his family. The hours went by fast and it was soon dark outside. Dionysius stopped the bus and let one of his helpers take the wheel while he lay down on the seat behind and easily fell asleep. I closed my eyes again and dreamed of cyclops throwing rocks and flash floods tearing down hillsides toward me.

I awoke with a start and realized that the bus had stopped, and we were sitting at the junction of the main north-south highway. One of the boys told me that this was my stop. They were going south to Lima, while I was going to Huaraz, to the hacienda where I had been staying before my trek into the mountains. I had left some belongings there and wanted to say goodbye to my new friends before I left the country.

Everyone was asleep, including Dionysius. So, I didn't have to go through any goodbyes except to the bus driver and his helpers. We smiled at each other and waved adios as I jumped off the bus into the early morning darkness.

The engine started back up and the smell of diesel filled my nostrils as the Condor de Chavín and the souls that it carried hit the smooth asphalt highway heading for Lima, another ten hours of easy driving away. I stood there, alone on the highway, and waited for another bus to take me on to Huaraz. A sense of peace filled me, knowing that these last few days in Peru were not soon to be forgotten.

El fin

REFERENCES

Peru in Four Dimensions, David A. Robinson 1964 American Studies. Press S.A. Lima, Peru (Out of Print)

These slides are known as Huaycos and are a common occurrence in the Sierras. They are a product of erosion on hillsides from heavy and prolonged rainfall, especially when vegetation is sparse. Instead of the normal flow of water to the valley floor, a mud flow or soil slump occurs, carrying large boulders and anything else in its way. At worst, Huaycos are mud avalanches that sweep down mountains and river beds, destroying everything in their path. There is no real protection against them, and repairs can't be made until the flow has ceased and stabilized.

Chavín de Huántar

Khan Academy

Chavín de Huántar is an archaeological and cultural site in the Andean highlands of Peru. Once thought to be the birthplace of an ancient "mother culture," the modern understanding is more nuanced. The cultural expressions found at Chavín most likely did not originate in that place, but can be seen as coming into their full force there. The visual legacy of Chavín would persist long after the site's decline in approximately 200 B.C.E., with motifs and stylistic elements traveling to the southern highlands and to the coast. The location of Chavín seems to have helped make it a special place—the temple built there became an important pilgrimage site that drew people and their offerings from far and wide.

At 10,330 feet (3150 meters) in elevation, it sits between the eastern (Cordillera Negra—snowless) and western (Cordillera Blanca—snowy) ranges of the Andes, near two of the few mountain passes that allow passage between the desert coast to the west and the Amazon jungle to the east. It is also located near the confluence of the Huachesca and Mosna Rivers, a natural phenomenon of two joining into one that may have been seen as a spiritually powerful phenomenon.

Over the course of 700 years, the site drew many worshipers to its temple who helped in spreading the artistic style of Chavín throughout highland and coastal Peru by transporting ceramics, textiles, and other portable objects back to their homes.

https://www.khanacademy.org/humanities/ap-art-history/indigenous-americas/a/Chavín-de-huantar1

ABOUT THE AUTHOR

When I was a young man, I wanted to see the world and took off after college in 1971. I bought a one-way ticket to Amsterdam and spent the next two and a half years traveling to far flung places. For two summers, I worked in Norway and then traveled overland to India-Nepal a couple of different times. It was an adventure that totally changed my perspective on the world.

As the years rolled by, my tire sales job in Oregon allowed me to take winters off. I visited Peru, Guatemala, Belize and much of Mexico. I've always liked spending time with the locals where I traveled and found that they enjoyed sharing their perspectives with me. The connections that I made on some of those travels have stood the test of time.

Eventually, I got married, and our family has made several trips to reconnect with treasured friends abroad. Lately, I've been spending more time following my wife as we visit our son and his family who have lived in Japan the past seven years. Who knows where the next trip will lead?

This story was written about 40 years ago, after a trip to Peru in 1979. It was an experience that left a flood of memories etched in my mind. I am confident that the reader will find it as entertaining as it was exhilarating.

Sam Woolsey
December 2018

41697425R00060

Made in the USA
Middletown, DE
09 April 2019